A Gift For

Cameron

_____

From

♡ Stacy

_____

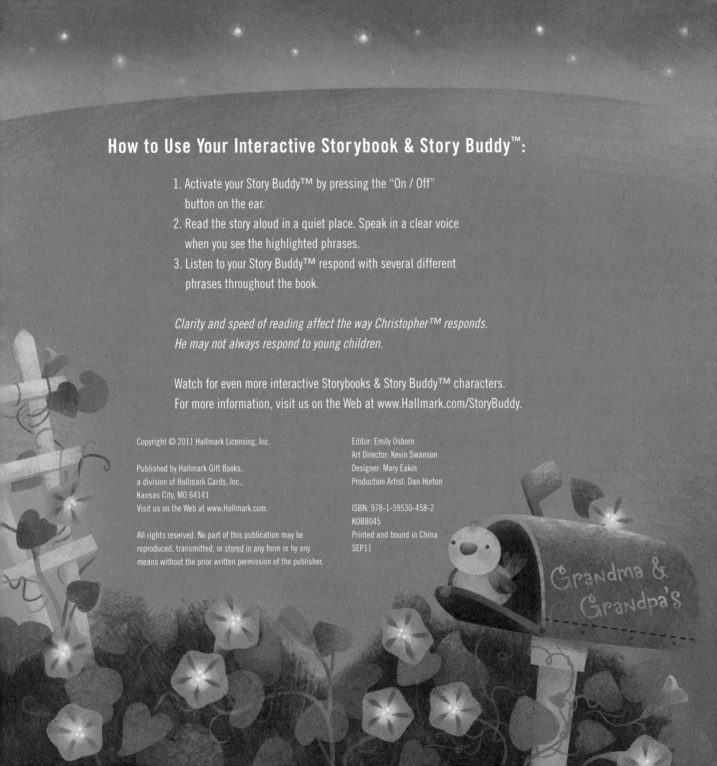

How to Use Your Interactive Storybook & Story Buddy™:

1. Activate your Story Buddy™ by pressing the "On / Off" button on the ear.
2. Read the story aloud in a quiet place. Speak in a clear voice when you see the highlighted phrases.
3. Listen to your Story Buddy™ respond with several different phrases throughout the book.

Clarity and speed of reading affect the way Christopher™ responds.
He may not always respond to young children.

Watch for even more interactive Storybooks & Story Buddy™ characters.
For more information, visit us on the Web at www.Hallmark.com/StoryBuddy.

Copyright © 2011 Hallmark Licensing, Inc.

Published by Hallmark Gift Books,
a division of Hallmark Cards, Inc.,
Kansas City, MO 64141
Visit us on the Web at www.Hallmark.com.

Editor: Emily Osborn
Art Director: Kevin Swanson
Designer: Mary Eakin
Production Artist: Dan Horton

ISBN: 978-1-59530-458-2
KOB8045
Printed and bound in China
SEP11

—— BOOK 2 ——

Christopher's
Night at Grandma
and Grandpa's

By **Megan Haave**
Illustrated by **Jeanne Rittmueller**

Hallmark
GIFT BOOKS

Christopher brushed his teeth and thought of all the fun he'd had that day with Grandma and Grandpa. He was spending the night at their house all by himself for the very first time.

Grandma and Grandpa tucked Christopher in and gave him good night kisses.

"Sweet, silly, super-duper dreams," said Grandpa. They turned off the light and shut the bedroom door behind them.

Christopher closed his eyes and tried to sleep.

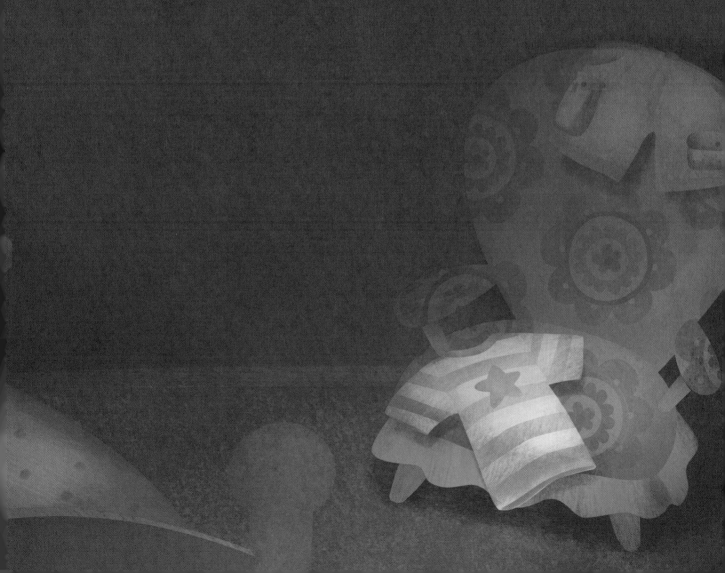

After lying there for a while, Christopher wasn't having sweet, silly, or any other kind of dreams. He loved being with Grandma and Grandpa, but he also missed home. Christopher had trouble falling asleep.

Christopher rolled over and reached toward the bedside table. He was feeling thirsty. But Christopher didn't find what he was looking for. At home, there was always a glass of water by his bed. Grandma and Grandpa must have forgotten.

Christopher called out for his grandparents.

Grandma came to check up on Christopher. He told her he was thirsty.
Grandma knew just what Christopher needed.

Christopher took a big sip of water. It did seem to make him feel a little better. Grandma left the room. Christopher closed his eyes and tried to sleep.

After a few minutes, Christopher got frustrated. He stared at the ceiling. He looked at the closet door, cracked open just a little. Christopher wasn't used to the shadows. They weren't like the shadows in his room at home.

Christopher called out for his grandparents.

This time, Grandpa came to check on Christopher.
Christopher told Grandpa about the shadows keeping him up.
Grandpa knew just what Christopher needed.

"Let's chase those shadows away with a little light. That should make it easier to sleep," Grandpa said.

With the night light on, Christopher did feel a little calmer. His head sunk heavily into his pillow. Grandpa wished Christopher sweet, silly, super-duper dreams one more time, then left the room. Christopher closed his eyes and tried to sleep.

Even with the glass of water nearby and the night light, Christopher still couldn't sleep. He rubbed his tired eyes and looked around the room at all of Grandma and Grandpa's things. It made him miss his things—his robot, Robbie, his collection of bouncy balls, and his Captain Oink poster. Christopher called out for his grandparents.

Grandma and Grandpa came again to see what was the matter. Christopher told them about Robbie and all the rest of the things he missed from home. All this worrying was making him tired.

Grandma and Grandpa knew just what Christopher needed.

"Your Dad used to sleep with this turtle. I bet it will help
you sleep, too," Grandma said as she snuggled the turtle
in next to Christopher.
"Do you know where a turtle lives?" Grandpa asked.
As he yawned, Christopher thought long and hard.

Christopher wasn't sure.

"Anywhere!" said Grandma. "A turtle lives in its shell, so wherever the turtle goes, its house goes with it." Christopher wished his house went with him. He hugged the turtle close to his chest. His eyelids were feeling heavier and heavier. Christopher was feeling really sleepy.

"You know what else?" said Grandpa. "You are kind of like a turtle."

"Really?" Christopher said in a hushed voice.

"Yes," Grandpa assured him. "Wherever you go, you carry a little bit of home with you. That includes when you come here."

Christopher smiled a sleepy smile. He liked the sound of that. For the first time all night, Christopher knew he would be able to fall asleep. He was already on his way. Sleeping was a whole lot easier when he felt at home.

Grandma kissed Christopher on the nose. "I love you, Christopher."

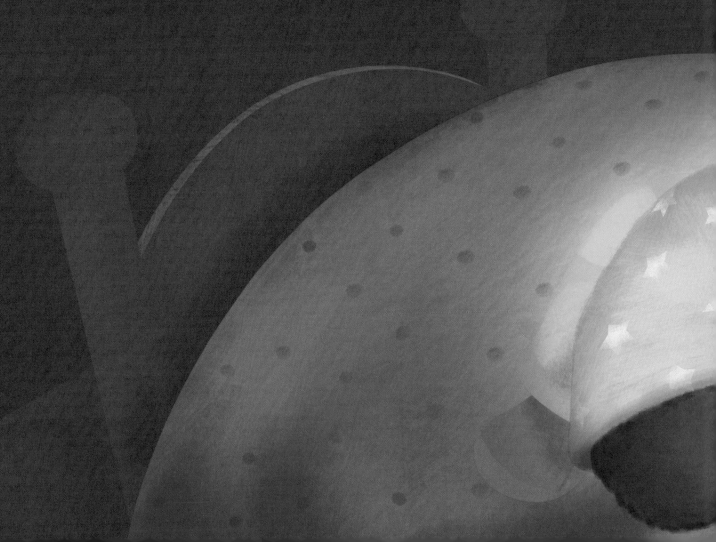

Grandma and Grandpa tucked in Christopher—and the turtle—one last time.

Christopher yawned a big yawn and his grandparents said, "Sweet dreams, Christopher."

Did you have fun reading with Christopher™?
We would love to hear from you!

Please send your comments to:
Hallmark Book Feedback
P.O. Box 419034
Mail Drop 215
Kansas City, MO 64141

Or e-mail us at:
booknotes@hallmark.com